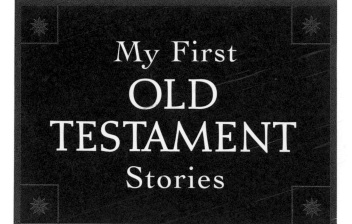

My First
**OLD
TESTAMENT**
Stories

This book belongs to

Presented by

Date

My First
OLD
TESTAMENT
Stories

Retold by Deanna Draper Buck
Illustrated by Jerry Harston

DESERET
BOOK

SALT LAKE CITY, UTAH

DESERET BOOK is a registered trademark of Deseret Book Company.

Visit us at DeseretBook.com

First printing in board book format 2001
First printing in paperbound 2010

ISBN-10 1-57345-960-7 (board book)
ISBN-13 978-1-57345-960-0 (board book)
ISBN-13 978-1-60641-689-1 (paperbound)

Printed in the United States of America 06/10
Artistic Printing, Salt Lake City, UT

10   9   8   7   6   5   4   3

To George, Stella, and Bonne Buck

Our Premortal Life

Long, long ago, before any of us were even born, we were all spirits. We lived together as brothers and sisters with our Heavenly Father. The time came when Heavenly Father told us that we were ready to go down to earth and receive bodies.

On earth we would learn how
to choose the right and to love
and help each other.

Jesus was chosen by Heavenly
Father to be the creator of a
beautiful world and to become
our Savior. We were so happy
that we all shouted for joy!

The Creation

Jesus made the world and everything in it. He made the mountains, the rivers and oceans, the clouds, the sun and moon and stars in the sky. He made all of the trees and plants and all of the animals.

When He was finished, the world was beautiful, and Heavenly Father said it was good.

Then Heavenly Father and Jesus created Adam and Eve, the first man and woman on the earth.

Adam and Eve

Adam and Eve lived in a beautiful place called the Garden of Eden. The Lord told them they could eat any of the fruit in the garden, except for the fruit of the Tree of Knowledge of Good and Evil. Satan was angry because he couldn't have a body, and he wanted to ruin God's plan. He tempted Adam and Eve to disobey Heavenly Father and eat the forbidden fruit. When they did so, Adam and Eve couldn't live in the Garden of Eden anymore.

Heavenly Father's Plan

After Adam and Eve left the Garden of Eden, an angel taught them about the Savior. The angel told them that if they would follow Jesus and live His teachings, then after Adam and Eve and their children died, they could all live with Heavenly Father again. Adam and Eve were happy to learn about the plan. They told their children about Jesus and taught them to love and help each other.

Noah

Noah was a prophet. He warned the people to obey God's commandments, but they would not listen to him. The Lord said He was going to destroy the wicked people and told Noah to build a large boat called an ark. Noah was told to take his family and two of each kind of animal into the ark.

Then it began to rain. Soon the earth was covered with water, but everyone on the ark was safe. After the flood was over, Heavenly Father made a rainbow in the sky as a sign He would never again cover the whole world with a flood.

The Tower of Babel

Many years after the flood, the world was filled with people once again. Some of the people were wicked and foolish. In their pride, they began to build a great city and a tower. They were not interested in the Lord or in keeping His commandments. The Lord was not happy with the people, and He confused their language so they couldn't talk to each other. He scattered them all over the world. A man named Jared and his family and friends loved the Lord, and their tongues were not confused. They were led by the Lord to the Americas, the promised land. You can read about them in the Book of Mormon.

Abraham and Isaac

Abraham loved his young son Isaac very much. One day the Lord told Abraham to sacrifice Isaac. Abraham did not want to do so, but he was obedient and took Isaac up a high mountain. Just as Abraham was ready to sacrifice Isaac, an angel stopped him. There was a sheep caught in some nearby bushes. Abraham sacrificed the sheep instead of Isaac. The angel told Abraham that the Lord was pleased with Abraham because he was willing to keep the commandments of God.

God's Covenant with Abraham

Because Abraham promised to love God and be obedient, the Lord made Abraham a special promise, called a covenant. Abraham was promised that Jesus would be born into Abraham's family;

that Abraham would have more people in his family
than there are stars in the sky or grains of sand on
the seashore; and that Abraham and his family would
hold the priesthood and bless the whole world.

Joseph

Joseph was a good boy who loved Heavenly Father and tried to do what was right. But his older brothers were jealous of Joseph, and one day they sold him to some men who were going to Egypt. They let their father believe that Joseph had been killed by a wild animal.

While Joseph was in Egypt, Pharaoh had a dream about a coming famine. The Lord helped Joseph understand the dream. Then Pharaoh asked Joseph to help store food so there would be no famine in Egypt.

Later, when Joseph's brothers came to Egypt to buy food, Joseph was happy to see them and forgave them for being unkind to him. He asked them to bring their father and their families to live in Egypt. Imagine how happy Joseph's father was to see him again.

Moses Is Born

Many years later, a new pharaoh of Egypt was afraid the Israelites were becoming stronger than the Egyptians, so he made a law to kill all the Israelite baby boys.

To save her baby boy, one mother made a basket and put her newborn son in it. She floated the basket on the river and told her daughter, Miriam, to hide in the reeds and watch what would happen.

Pharaoh's daughter found the basket with the baby in it. She saved the baby and took care of him. She named him Moses, and the boy grew up a prince in Pharaoh's palace.

God Speaks to Moses

After Moses grew up, he left Egypt to live in the land of Midian. There the Lord spoke to Moses from a burning bush. The Israelites had become slaves, and God told Moses to tell Pharaoh to let the Israelites go. But Pharaoh said, "No!" Then the Lord sent plagues and sickness and death to the Egyptians. Finally, Pharaoh told Moses he could take the children of Israel and leave Egypt.

Crossing the Red Sea

Moses led the children of Israel out of
Egypt. They crossed a desert and finally
came to the Red Sea. Moses prayed,
and the Lord parted the waters of the
sea so the people could cross on dry ground.
When Pharaoh's army tried to follow them
and bring them back to Egypt, the sea closed
up and drowned the soldiers. The children
of Israel were safe, and they thanked the
Lord for saving them from their enemies.

The Ten Commandments

One day the Lord led Moses to a high mountain called Sinai, where He gave Moses some special laws called the Ten Commandments.

The Ten Commandments taught the people to love and obey Heavenly Father, to love their parents, and to be honest and kind to one another. The Lord promised them that obeying the commandments would help them to be happy.

Joshua

After Moses died, the Lord made Joshua the leader of the children of Israel. Joshua led the people into the promised land. The people who were already living there were wicked. Joshua told the Israelites that before they entered the promised land, they needed to decide whether or not they would serve Heavenly Father. Joshua said that he and his family would serve the Lord. The Israelites also promised that they would obey Heavenly Father.

The Battle of Jericho

The Israelites had to conquer the promised land before they could live there.
The first city they came to was
Jericho. There were high
walls around the
city.

The Lord told Joshua to tell the people to march around Jericho every day for six days. Then on the seventh day they were to march around the city seven times and the priests were to blow their trumpets while everyone shouted. The people did as Joshua commanded, and the walls of Jericho fell down. The Israelites won the battle and were able to enter the promised land.

Jonah and the Whale

The Lord called Jonah on a mission to the wicked
city of Nineveh, but Jonah was afraid to go. He de-
cided to get on a boat and run away.
There was a bad storm on the sea. Jonah
realized the Lord was unhappy with him
and told the sailors to throw him into
the stormy sea.

God sent a large fish to swallow Jonah. After three days inside the fish, Jonah repented and promised to go on his mission. The big fish spit him out on the beach, and Jonah hurried to Nineveh. He taught the people the gospel, and they repented of their sins. Jonah had become a good missionary.

Hannah and Samuel

While Hannah was at the temple praying to have a child, she was promised by Eli the priest that God would answer her prayer. When her baby was born, Hannah was so thankful that she promised to give him back to the Lord. When Samuel was old enough, she took him to the temple to be a helper for Eli. One night the boy Samuel heard a voice calling him. He thought it was Eli, but it was the Lord, calling Samuel to be a prophet. Samuel listened to the Lord and obeyed Him.

The Lord Chooses a King for Israel

The Lord sent the prophet Samuel to call one of Jesse's sons to be the new king of Israel. All of Jesse's sons were strong and handsome, but the Lord told Samuel not to pay attention to how they looked on the outside. When Samuel looked at some of Jesse's sons, he knew the Lord had not chosen one of them. "Do you have any other sons?" he asked. Jesse sent for his youngest son, David, who was tending the sheep. When Samuel saw David, he knew the Lord had chosen the boy to be the king. David had a good heart and loved Heavenly Father.

David and Goliath

The Philistines were at war with the Israelites. The Philistines had a giant named Goliath in their army. Every day Goliath would shout, "Send someone to fight me!" No one dared to fight a giant. But when young David heard Goliath's challenge, David asked the king for permission to fight the giant. David told the king that the Lord had already helped him kill a lion and a bear that had tried to eat David's sheep. David did not have a sword or armor. The only weapon he had was a sling shot and five smooth stones. Because David had so much faith, the Lord helped him kill the giant Goliath and save the army of Israel.

Daniel in the Lions' Den

Daniel was King Darius's trusted helper. Some of the king's other helpers were jealous of Daniel and tricked the king into making a law that everyone must pray to the king instead of to God. These wicked men knew that Daniel prayed three times a day to Heavenly Father and that he would not pray to the king. They waited and watched until they found Daniel saying his prayers. Then they put Daniel into a den of lions. The king was sorry that he had made the law. He fasted and worried all night, hoping that his friend Daniel would be safe. In the morning, the king hurried to see what had happened to Daniel.

Daniel was safe. The Lord had sent an angel to protect Daniel from the hungry lions.

Queen Esther

Esther was a young Israelite woman who lived in Persia. The king of Persia chose Esther to be his queen because she was good and kind as well as beautiful. One of the king's helpers didn't like the Israelites. The king didn't know Queen Esther was an Israelite and was tricked by the wicked Haman into making a law to have the Israelites killed. Esther and all the Israelites fasted and prayed for three days, then Esther begged the king to spare her and her people. Haman was punished, and the Israelites thanked the Lord for Esther's courage and for saving them.

Elijah and the Widow

Elijah was a prophet. When a famine came in the land, Elijah stayed in the mountains by a little stream. God sent ravens twice a day with some food for Elijah. After the stream dried up, Elijah went to a tiny village and asked a poor widow there for some food. She had just enough flour and oil to make bread for her and her son. Then their food would be gone. But she shared what she had with the prophet. Elijah promised her that she would have flour and oil for the rest of the famine. God blessed her for sharing.

Naaman and Elisha

Naaman was a leader in the Syrian army. He was a good man, but he had a terrible skin disease called leprosy. A young Israelite girl, who was a maid in his house, told Naaman that Elisha the prophet could cure his leprosy. When Naaman went to visit Elisha, the prophet told him to wash seven times in the Jordan River. Naaman didn't think that would help and started to go home. But his friends said, "If the prophet had told you to do something hard, you would have done it, but you think this is too easy."

Naaman was sorry his faith had been so weak and obeyed Elisha. His leprosy was healed! He was blessed because he listened to the prophet.

Malachi

Malachi was the last Old Testament prophet. He promised that the Lord will open the windows of heaven and bless us if we will pay our tithing. Paying tithing shows Heavenly Father that we are thankful for our blessings and that we believe in Him.

Malachi also taught that the prophet Elijah would come in the last days to plant in the hearts of the children the promises made to the fathers, and that the hearts of the children would turn to their fathers. Elijah appeared to Joseph Smith in the Kirtland Temple and gave him the sealing power. Families who are sealed in the temple can be together forever.

About the Author

Award-winning, bestselling author Deanna Draper Buck and her husband have been married over forty years. They currently live in Hooper, Utah, where they enjoy gardening, the Great Salt Lake, and entertaining their nineteen grandchildren. Deanna has written nine LDS children's books, explaining gospel principles, Church history, and scriptures stories in a simplified style.

About the Illustrator

Jerry Harston held a degree in graphic design and illustrated more than thirty children's books. He received many honors for his art, and his clients included numerous Fortune 500 corporations. Jerry passed away in December 2009.